Defining Your Destiny for Success:

Techniques for Unlocking Your Intellect

By

Chigozirim Clinton Okoroafor

TABLE OF CONTENTS

Introduction:

How do you measure success? Are you happy after you've achieved your work goals? Financial goals? given them an education, What about when you can leave without having to worry about money?

Everyone has a different way of describing success. Yet, why do so many people feel that their life is a failure?

One of the most important steps to reaching success in life is to understand the meaning of success for your own life. The real meaning of success goes much beyond the usual ideas of success, such as having a lot of money, being wealthy, having a lot of tangibles, and getting degrees. Quite the opposite: real success in life cannot be judged with the above-named elements, but instead with the number of individuals who can live a better and more developed life because of what you made. This is the meaning of success. Not the awards people are collecting in their lives. Media and society allow us to frequently believe that living a happy life includes being enormously rich and having a lot of tangibles. But the meaning of success is to live a happy life and to make this world a better place for everyone. It is having the confidence to

follow one's own way when pushed by the fear of
the unknown.

So, have you been looking at success incorrectly? Have
you viewed success as something to be gained rather than
something to be given? A life well spent is one dedicated,
not to the chase of others' praise, but to the betterment of
their lives

Chapter 1: What is Success

Being successful implies the realization of desired visions
and planned objectives. Furthermore, success may be a
specific social standing that characterizes a successful
individual who might also have achieved a reputation for
its beneficial conclusion.

One of the most crucial stages to achieving success in life
is to recognize the meaning of success for your own life.
The genuine meaning of success extends much beyond
the traditional conceptions of success, such as having a lot
of money, being affluent, having a lot of tangibles, and
receiving degrees. Quite the opposite: genuine success in
life cannot be judged with the above-named elements, but
instead with the number of individuals who can live a
better and more evolved life because of what you made.
This is the meaning of success. Not the trophies
individuals are accumulating in their lives. Media and
culture allow us to frequently believe that living a
successful life involves being enormously rich and

possessing a lot of tangibles. But the meaning of success is to live a happy life and to make this planet a better place for everyone.

What is the meaning of success? Success may be characterized in two ways — the broad sense and the precise sense. In the broader meaning, success is the completion of a stated objective. There are several consequences of this definition. The first implication is that you accomplish success anytime you can transfer a specified aim into reality. Another consequence of this notion is that success inevitably implies achievement. Hence, there is nothing like partial success. Another consequence of this definition of success, which is highly essential, is that success is necessarily tied to a specified objective. Hence, you cannot achieve a goal you did not establish.

How do you define success? Are you successful after you've attained your professional goals? Financial goals? Are you successful after you have reared your kids, given them an education, and paid for their weddings? What about when you can retire without having to worry about money?

Everyone has a distinct method of defining success. Yet, why do so many people feel that their life is a failure? When you spend your life committed to loving and helping others, you are, indeed, successful."

Defining your destiny for success

As you'll read, success has nothing to do with attaining a monetary amount, obtaining a promotion, or any other usual meaning of the term. But, first, let me suggest two circumstances, and you judge whether each person is a success:

Sophie has been working full-time as a project manager for a big new endeavor at her business. All project goals have been met on time and within budget. Yet, after two years, the corporation decided to discontinue the project and halt all work on it. Is Sophie a success?

Joseph has been working his whole career to become vice president of sales at a prominent corporation. Finally, after 22 years, he has fulfilled his aim. He is now earning more money than he ever believed imaginable, but the position necessitates that he travels widely and works over 70 hours each week. Consequently, Joseph's wife has filed for divorce, and his two kids scarcely recognize him. Is Joseph a success?

One could argue that they are successful for Sophie and Joseph. On the other hand, you could make a case that each has yet to be effective for several reasons.
Let's study the meaning of success from three crucial perspectives: from our viewpoint, from the viewpoint of others, and from God's perspective.

Each is significant in one way or another, but each symbolizes an important component of our lives that cannot be disregarded when we look at five crucial questions: Am I successful now? What has to change for me to become successful? At the end of my life, what will decide whether my life was successful?

Success from our standpoint

When I look at the lives of successful people and seek to define traits of success, I believe there are just three things to ask:

1. → Did they do the best they could in the times and conditions of their lives?

2. → Did they have a good effect on the lives of their family, friends, colleagues, and community?

1. → Did they leave behind a legacy of peace, happiness, love, and encouragement?

You'll note that the three "markers" for success have nothing to do with the size of their home, vacations, vehicles, and titles. The way success is judged is whether you made use of the chance you are given to affect people positively and whether you left behind good or bad. Certainly, even much of this is subjective. But you can assess success in these areas by whether friends and family love your company and desire to be with you. You can know for sure if you helped enhance the careers or lives of others.

Certainly, one component of this opinion is whether you did your best for your family. Providing a steady and healthy living is crucial. Providing possibilities for education, pleasure, and enjoyment is important. Enjoying life and experiencing a sense of success should be essential objectives for all of us. However, too many make this their major purpose in life. Pursuing self-happiness at the cost of all others and all other pursuits is typically the basis of unhappiness and lack of satisfaction. Finding a balance that satisfies your essential personal duties but gives abundant opportunity to enrich the lives of others is that puzzle piece that we all aspire to discover.

Success from the standpoint of others

Too many of us spend our lives trying too hard to satisfy or impress others. Though you may never know for sure how others consider success in your life, these three questions could help guide your thoughts and actions about actual success in their eyes:

1. → When people think about me, does it make them smile?

2. → When people think about me, do they believe that their life is better because they know me?

3. → When people think of me, are they driven to make a difference for someone else because of the example I left behind?

 When a loved one dies, you can recall that no one talks about that person's monetary prosperity. The chats are usually about pleasant times, wonderful recollections, and what they did (or didn't do) for others. You know, in the end, we all assess a good life by how it was lived, not by what was accumulated.

When you think of successful persons, a consistent component in each is how they try to lift someone up to a higher level of success. They constantly contributed more than they received. They demonstrated a feeling of delight because they were secure in who they were rather than a sense of anxiety because of who they were not. You see, success emits a feeling of happiness and confidence that draws people, not repels them.

Success from God's viewpoint

The most essential area of achievement in life is from the standpoint of God. After all, if you believe in God, you know that our connection with Him, in the end, decides our everlasting destiny. According to the Bible, what defines a successful life according to God:

1. → Did I establish peace with God by embracing Jesus as my Lord and Savior?

2. → Did I display my love for God by sharing my love with others?

3. → Was my life defined by constant and persistent progress in knowledge, love, service, and commitment to God?

To be clear, we cannot labor our way to peace with God. We are incapable. Jesus, however, was sent by God to redeem us. Jesus' death on the cross, in our place, settled our debt and provided our bridge back to God. Success in God's sight is embracing the gift of everlasting life offered by Jesus' sacrifice on the cross. And, as a consequence of embracing Him, our life becomes a live manifestation of God's love for us via the love we share with others. No life can be genuinely judged as successful until we have achieved this peace with God.

So, have you been looking at success incorrectly? Have you considered success as something to be earned rather than something to be given? A life well spent is one committed, not to the chase of others' admiration, but to the betterment of their lives.

Chapter 2: The Self Concept

Self-idea is the image we've got of ourselves. It is impacted by way of diverse causes, including our dating with key individuals in our lifestyles. It is how we see our activities, abilities, and one-of-a-kind features. For example, ideas that include "I am a terrific person" or "I am a kind person" are part of a usual self-idea. Our self-perception is crucial since it impacts our motives, attitudes, and actions. It also impacts how we experience the person we accept as true as we are, inclusive of whether or not we're in a position or have self-esteem.

Defining your destiny for success

Self-concept is extra changeable while we are younger and still going through self-discovery and identity creation. As we mature and understand who we are and what is crucial to us, those self-perceptions emerge as an awful lot more particular and ordered. At its most fundamental, self-concept is a hard and fast of ideas one has about oneself and the reactions of others. It gives the response to the query, "Who am I"? List gadgets that represent you as a person if you need to find out yourself-idea.;. What are your tendencies? What do you want? How do you feel about yourself? Humanist psychologist Carl Rogers argued that self-concept is made of 3 fundamental components:

- The ideal self
- The self-image
- The self-esteem

Ideal self: The Ideal self is the person you aspire to be. This person possesses the traits or qualities you are both striving closer to or choosing to own. It's who you see yourself to be. The "; Ideal self" refers to the version of oneself that a person wishes to turn out to be. It is a depiction of the attributes, characteristics, ideals, and behaviors that someone considers because they are first-class or most suited for oneself. The ideal self is commonly impacted by using cultural requirements, social expectations, private goals, and man or woman goals. Here are a few cruise social factors to comprehend about the suitable self:

Defining your destiny for success

 Aspirational Nature: The ideal self symbolizes the person's ambitions and pursuits for personal increase and improvement. It might also cowl traits together with self-assurance, kindness, success, mind, or other elements that the individual admires or appreciates.

Motivation and Drive: People are usually driven with the aid of choice to bridge the space between their gift self (how they view themselves today) and their perfect self. This purpose can also drive behavior and selections as humans are looking to suit their behaviors with their favored self-photograph.

Influence of Society and Culture: Cultural and sociological elements have a vital component in growing one's ideal self. Cultural norms and cultural standards decide whether attributes are seen as suited or respectable in positive surroundings.

Psychological Impact: The pursuit of the right self also has psychological implications. When people agree that they may be coming closer to their first-rate selves, they will revel in a feeling of fulfillment and higher vanity. On the other hand, if the space between the actual self and the pleasant self is considered tremendous, it might cause feelings of discontent or horrible self-esteem.
Flexibility and Change: The ideal self is not a

difficult and fast notion. It may additionally adjust through the years as human beings develop, observe, and alter to new life situations. What a person considers their high-quality self in their adolescence may also want to regulate as they reap new insights and goals.

<u>Striving for Balance</u>: While chasing the exceptional self may be inspiring, it is essential to create a balance between self-development and self-reputation. Unrealistic or too strict necessities may bring about tension and unhappiness. Embracing one's strengths and spotting shortcomings is also a vital detail of a wholesome self-idea.

Overall, the suitable self affords an imaginative and prescient personal perfection that affects human beings' goals and behaviors. It's a dynamic idea that depicts human evolution and the ordinary quest for self-discovery.

Self-image: Self-image refers to the way you view yourself at this factor. Attributes, including physical attributes, mental tendencies, and social positions, all play a part in your self-image.

Self-image refers to the mental and emotional view that someone has of themselves. It accommodates how someone perspectives oneself in terms of bodily looks, persona traits, talents, and different aspects.

Self-image is stricken by both inner variables (together with private thoughts and emotions) and external factors (consisting of social interactions and comments from others).

Here are some important factors to grasp regarding self-image:

Subjective Perception: Self-image is a subjective angle that a person maintains about themselves. It may or may not be in shape with how others view them. It's about a person's perspective and is familiar with themselves, such as their strengths, faults, and standard identity.

Multidimensional: Self-image is multidimensional and incorporates numerous aspects of one's identity. This might encompass bodily appearance (frame photograph), social roles, highbrow capacity, emotional qualities, and more. These traits make contributions to the entire self-concept.

Influences: Self-image is impacted by a large number of factors, including cultural norms, social requirements of attractiveness, upbringing, stories, media depictions, and relationships with one's own family, buddies, and friends. Positive or poor entry from others can also affect how a person perceives themselves.

Self-esteem: Self-image is strongly tied to vanity, which is the whole opinion and mindset a person has about themselves. A desirable self-picture is generally associated with extended shallowness, whereas a negative self-photo may additionally contribute to reduced shallowness.

.

<u>Dynamic and Malleable</u>: Self-image isn't always set; it could range over the years, relying on new stories, non-public development, and changes in self-belief. Individuals can also modify their self-image once they accomplish goals, overcome issues, or take advantage of new competencies.

<u>Cognitive Conflict</u>: When there's an enormous difference between one's self-image and truth, it could lead to cognitive dissonance — a psychological soreness created via discrepancies among ideals and behaviors. People may additionally sense tension or a desire to suit their moves with their self-image.

<u>Positive Self-Image</u>: Cultivating a positive self-image involves spotting and appreciating one's strengths, embracing shortcomings, and cultivating wholesome self-esteem. Positive self-affirmations, self-care habits, and looking for assistance from others may also cause an extra fine self-picture.

In summary, self-image is a complicated and comprehensive mental assembly that plays a key role in determining a person's thoughts, feelings, movements, and preferred well-being. It's a fundamental part of self-idea and identity introduction.

Self-esteem: How a great deal you like, be given, and appreciate yourself all make contributions to your self-idea. Self-esteem may be impacted by way of different factors—along with how human beings view you and your function in society. Self-esteem refers to the subjective appraisal, attitude, and trendy opinion that a person has about their real worth, fee, and skills. It suggests the diploma of confidence, respect, and recognition a person feels for oneself. Self-esteem determines how people regard themselves and how they interact with the world around them. Here are some vital elements to grasp regarding self-esteem:

<u>Subjective Evaluation:</u> Self-esteem is a non-public evaluation that people make about themselves. It's based totally on their private perspectives, thoughts, and feelings, approximately their competency, likability, and relevance.

<u>Positive and Negative Self-Esteem:</u> Positive vanity incorporates having a fine self-view, where humans know their strengths, take delivery of their limitations, and believe in their abilities. Negative vanity, on the other side, encompasses emotions of self-doubt, inadequacy, and a loss of confidence.

Defining your destiny for success

Influences: Self-esteem is impacted through various variables, along with early life occasions, parental aid and recognition, social interactions, successes, failures, and private stories. Positive feedback and reinforcement from others may additionally boost vanity, as terrible stories can erode it.

Effect on Behavior: Self-esteem can also dramatically affect how human beings behave. Those with more shallowness have a tendency to address problems with self-assurance, take healthful risks, and hold stronger relationships. In assessment, bad shallowness can also result in avoidance of problems, social isolation, and difficulty in exerting oneself.

Developmental Aspect: Self-esteem often develops in the course of infancy and early life; however, it continues to trade for the duration of adulthood. Early studies and the signals human beings soak up from their surroundings may additionally impact their self-esteem for years to come.

Self-Efficacy: A comparable notion is self-efficacy, which is the perception of one's ability to perform precise sports or goals. High self-efficacy can also cause multiplied shallowness, as folks who assume they're capable of achievement are much more likely to have true self-views.

Balanced Self-Esteem: Balanced self-esteem is a practical and wholesome self-assessment that accepts both strengths and faults. It's now not about arrogance or perfectionism but about having a worrying and straightforward view of oneself.

Nurturing Self-Esteem: Developing and nurturing proper vanity involves practicing self-compassion, setting up affordable goals, spotting triumphs, and getting help whilst required. Challenging bad self-speak and engaging in self-care may help to more self-esteem.

In summary, self-esteem is an essential part of mental well-being that determines how people experience themselves and the way they connect to their surroundings. Cultivating healthful and top shallowness is essential for private development, resilience, and average lifestyle pleasure.

Now, you must be questioning, how do these things assist me to attain success? Well, in case you examine beneath, you'll find out that the self-concept could be essential to acquiring fulfillment. Let us look at how every part of the self-concept contributes to achievement.

Ideal Self:

Motivation: The ideal self displays the character you try to be, your aspirations, and your photo of your exceptional self. Having a corporate grasp of your ideal self might encourage you to strive toward becoming that man or woman. Success normally includes defining and pursuing significant targets related to your best self.

Goal defining: The perfect self also functions as a compass for defining practical goals. Success is commonly the final result of making and operating towards these goals, which are guided by your ideal self.

Personal development: Continuously looking to connect your behaviors together with your best self might also cause private improvement and self-improvement, which can be crucial for lengthy-time period fulfillment. It's approximately developing and getting higher over time.

Self-Esteem:

Confidence: Self-esteem is your entire feeling of self-esteem and self-belief in your talents. High vanity offers the confidence required to take on problems, discover opportunities, and bear within the face of adversity, all of which are essential for fulfillment.

Resilience: People with robust vanity are regularly more resilient. They can bounce back from setbacks and disappointments, thinking about them as transitory setbacks instead of as reflections in their price. This resilience is vital to obtaining achievement.

Positive Relationships: Self-esteem also influences how you interact with others. Building and preserving splendid connections is often essential in several facets of lifestyles and can open doors to fulfillment.

Self-Image:

Self-Perception: Your self-image is the way you view yourself, along with your strengths, shortcomings, and widespread identity. An exact self-image may help you recognize your capability and abilities, which can be critical for growing and reaching objectives.

Self-Confidence: A suitable self-photograph also improves self-belief, making it less complicated to take possibilities and explore possibilities. It could also impact how human beings view and react to you, opening doors to achievement.

<u>Self-satisfying prophesy</u>: Your self-picture might end up a self-fulfilling prophecy. If you regard yourself as in a position and successful character, you are more inclined to take part in movements that lead to success. As you can see, the appropriate self, self-esteem, and self-image are interwoven aspects of 1's self-concept that may substantially make a contribution to fulfillment. Having a clear photo of your ideal self might also force and direct your sports, while high vanity can come up with the self-belief and resilience required to stand issues.

An excellent self-image forms your attitude toward your competencies and has an effect on how others see you, subsequently affecting your route toward success. Cultivating these components of yourself-concept may be crucial elements in accomplishing your objectives and dreams.

Chapter 3: Relationship Between Ego and Intellect

Before we discuss the link between ego and intellect, let us establish a clear description of what these words entail.

The Ego: The ego is a psychological notion that derives from psychoanalytic theory, notably the work of Sigmund Freud. It is one of the three components of the human mind, together with the "Id" (ID, the innate unconscious

component of personality that is present from birth, is the basis of physiological urges and demands as well as emotional compulsions.) and the super-ego. The ego symbolizes the conscious and intellectual component of the mind that mediates between the primal urges of the "id" and the moral limitations of the super-ego.
Here are crucial aspects to grasp about the ego:

<u>Mediation:</u> The ego works as a mediator between the opposing desires of the "id" and the super-ego. The "id" functions on the pleasure principle, seeking immediate fulfillment of cravings and instincts, whereas the super-ego embodies society's standards and moral principles. The ego's task is to find a balance between these contending forces

.

<u>Reality Testing:</u> Reality testing is done by the ego. It helps humans navigate the actual world by examining the feasibility and repercussions of their objectives and behaviors. It evaluates the external facts and social standards before acting on urges.

<u>Decision-Making</u>: The ego participates in decision-making processes. It examines alternative possibilities, considers possible dangers and advantages, and makes decisions that meet both the "id's" wants and the super-ego's moral concerns.

<u>Conscious Awareness</u>: Unlike the "id", which functions predominantly at an unconscious level, and the super-ego, which integrates moral ideals, the ego operates mostly in conscious awareness. It helps people comprehend and interpret their experiences from the perspective of reality.

<u>Defense Mechanisms:</u> The ego utilizes defense mechanisms to deal with anxiety and conflicts originating from the demands of the "id" and the super-ego. These strategies include processes like suppression, denial, projection, and rationalization, which assist in regulating internal conflicts.

<u>Development</u>: Freud claimed that the ego develops early in infancy when a kid learns to deal with the demands of the external environment. It grows increasingly complex as people mature and interact with their surroundings. Freud is the founder of psychoanalysis, which is a clinical method for evaluating and treating pathologies. Pathology is a branch of medicine concerned with the cause, origin, and nature of diseases, including changes occurring as a result of diseases.

<u>Identity and Self:</u> The ego is directly related to an individual's sense of self and personal identity. It helps develop a coherent and consistent self-concept based on experiences, relationships, and self-perceptions.

<u>Psychoanalysis:</u> In psychoanalysis, the examination of the ego's functioning is vital to understanding a person's mental and emotional well-being. Treatments generally entail analyzing how the ego controls conflicts, defenses, and coping mechanisms.

The Intellect: Intellect refers to the ability to think, comprehend, and obtain knowledge. It covers cognitive talents that entail critical thinking, logical analysis, problem-solving, and abstract cognition. The intellect is a key feature of human cognition that allows humans to absorb information, make decisions, and participate in complicated cognitive activities.

Here are crucial elements to comprehend regarding intellect:

<u>Reasoning:</u> Intellect includes the capacity to think rationally and generate conclusions based on available knowledge. It involves deductive reasoning (drawing particular conclusions from general principles) and inductive reasoning (developing general principles from specific observations).

<u>Analysis:</u> The intellect permits humans to examine complicated circumstances, ideas, and facts. It involves breaking down information into smaller components to grasp their linkages and ramifications better.

Problem-Solving: Problem-solving is a crucial part of cognition. It entails recognizing difficulties, producing solutions, analyzing possibilities, and choosing the most suitable course of action.

Abstract Thinking: Abstract thinking is the capacity to grasp thoughts and ideas that may not have a clear, tangible manifestation in the physical world. It includes comprehending symbolic, metaphorical, or theoretical notions.

Learning: The intellect plays a crucial part in the process of learning. It lets humans learn new information, combine it with current knowledge, and adapt to new conditions.

Adaptability: The ability to adjust to changing circumstances depends on intellectual flexibility. Individuals with significant intellectual skills may modify their thoughts and conduct depending on new facts or difficulties.

Creativity: In creativity, an individual requires imaginative thinking, which depends on the intellect to develop, plan, and execute creative ideas in a cohesive and meaningful manner.

<u>Cognitive growth</u>: The growth of intelligence develops throughout life. Early childhood experiences and schooling contribute to the evolution of cognitive talents, and intellectual capabilities may continue to expand and improve through different phases of life.

<u>Influence on Decision-Making</u>: The intellect affects decision-making by providing the cognitive processes required to assess choices, foresee consequences, and pick a course of action.

<u>Cultural and Individual Differences:</u> The display of intelligence may differ among cultures and people. Different communities and environments may prioritize certain intellectual capabilities, and people may have varied strengths and preferences in their cognitive abilities.

In essence, intelligence covers a spectrum of cognitive skills that are necessary for reasoning, problem-solving, and learning. It is a key feature of human cognition that determines how humans interact with the environment, make choices, and participate in intellectual activities.

The Relationship Between Ego and Intellect

The link between ego and intellect resides in how they contribute to an individual's cognition, self-awareness, and decision-making processes. While these notions are unique, they frequently interact and impact each other in the following ways:

<u>Mediation and Decision-Making:</u> The ego, as defined in Freudian philosophy, plays a function in mediating between the primary urges of the "id" and the moral limitations of the super-ego. Fraud believes that the mind is responsible for both conscious and unconscious decisions that it makes on the basis of psychological drives. The id, ego, and super-ego are the three aspects of the mind Freud believed to comprise a person's personality. The ego involves reasonable and realistic thinking to establish a balance between instant enjoyment and cultural values. The intellect, on the other hand, gives the cognitive skills for logical analysis, critical thinking, and problem-solving. Together, the ego's mediating role and the intellect's decision-making skills enable humans to negotiate difficult circumstances, weighing both wishes and logical concerns.

<u>Reality Testing and Logical Analysis:</u> The ego's role in reality testing entails examining circumstances objectively and interpreting external reality. This incorporates cognitive processes that are strongly tied to the intellect's ability in logical thinking, critical analysis, and recognizing cause-and-effect connections. These cognitive processes help the ego's attempts to regulate urges and make well-informed judgments.

<u>Self-Awareness and Reflection:</u> The ego is related to an individual's sense of self, identity, and self-awareness. It helps build a cohesive self-concept. The intellect helps self-awareness by helping people to reflect on their ideas, feelings, actions, and experiences. This contemplation, facilitated by intellectual processes, adds to a greater knowledge of oneself, contributing to personal development and self-improvement.

<u>Coping and Defense Mechanisms:</u> The ego develops defense mechanisms to deal with conflicts emanating from the "id" and super-ego. These strategies generally include cognitive processes that either distort reality or assist in the control of anxiety. For instance, rationalization, a defensive mechanism, includes utilizing logical reasons to explain the action. These cognitive methods are impacted by the relationship between ego and intellect.

<u>Balancing Emotional and Intellectual replies:</u> The ego must balance emotional reactions with intellectual replies. The intellect contributes by helping humans assess emotional events, control emotional impulses, and make choices based on a mix of intellectual and emotional factors.

<u>Development and Growth:</u> Both the ego and intellect evolve and mature throughout time. As cognitive powers grow, the ego gets more skilled at resolving disputes and

making complicated judgments. The intellect's evolution adds to a more sophisticated view of oneself and the environment, which might impact how the ego navigates diverse circumstances.

In summation, the ego and intellect are interwoven in their roles and interactions within an individual's psychological processes. While the ego controls internal conflicts and balances impulses with logical considerations, the intellect gives the cognitive skills for analysis, decision-making, self-awareness, and personal progress. Their dynamic interaction contributes to an individual's cognitive performance, self-perception, and behavior.

Now, how do ego and intellect contribute to success? Ego and intellect may both play roles in obtaining success, but their influence on achievement might vary depending on how they are balanced and utilized. Let's analyze their relationship:

Ego:

As said earlier, ego refers to a person's feeling of self-esteem, self-importance, and self-identity. It frequently entails a need to be acknowledged, complimented, and affirmed. Ego may affect achievement in the following ways:

<u>Stimulate Ambition</u>: A healthy ego may stimulate ambition and push people to strive for achievement. It might motivate people to set lofty objectives and work hard to accomplish them.

<u>Confidence</u>: Ego may create a degree of self-confidence that is crucial for success. Believing in oneself and one's ability may lead to taking measured risks and grabbing chances.

<u>Resilience</u>: A well-balanced ego may help people bounce back from setbacks and disappointments. It keeps them from being easily disheartened by problems.
However, an enormous ego, marked by arrogance, selfishness, and contempt for others, may be harmful to success. It may lead to interpersonal disputes, intolerance to criticism, and poor decision-making.

Intellect:

As mentioned earlier, intellect refers to a person's cognitive talents, including thinking, problem-solving, learning, and adaptation. Intellectual qualities may contribute to success in the following ways:

<u>Problem-Solving</u>: Intellectual talents help people to assess difficult circumstances, make educated judgments, and

solve issues successfully. This is vital in numerous facets of life and profession.

Innovation: A high intellect may inspire creativity and innovation, which can lead to innovative ideas and solutions. Innovators typically find success by questioning the established status quo.

Continuous Learning: Intellectual curiosity and a desire to learn are vital for personal development and adaptability to changing circumstances. Success generally demands remaining current and adaptive.

Adaptability: Intellect helps people adjust to new problems, technology, and settings, which is crucial in today's fast-changing world.

In the end, ego and intellect may both contribute to success, but they need to be balanced. A large ego may inhibit success by alienating people and hindering personal progress, whereas a strong intellect can give the skills required to attain success via effective problem-solving and adaptability. The ideal strategy is to create a healthy ego that offers drive and confidence while utilizing one's intellect for competent and careful decision-making.

Chapter 4: Building Confidence

What is Confidence

Confidence is a mental condition defined by way of a strong conviction in a single's skills, attributes, and judgments. It consists of a feeling of self-assuredness and positive self-regard that helps people approach difficulties, duties, and encounters with an experience of poise and fact.

Confidence is not something that can be discovered as a fixed of guidelines; self-belief is a state of thought. Positive questioning, exercise education, and speaking to different humans arc all powerful strategies to help enhance or raise your self-belief ranges.
Confidence stems from emotions of being, the popularity of your frame and mind (your shallowness), and confidence in your capacity, abilities, and revel in.
Confidence is a trait that most individuals need to own.

What is Self-Confidence?

Although self-confidence may mean various things to different individuals, it just means having trust in yourself.
Confidence is, in part, a product of how we have been brought up and how we've been taught. We learn from others how to think about ourselves and how to act - these teachings influence what we believe about ourselves and

other people. Confidence is also a function of our experiences and how we've learned to respond to various circumstances.

Self-confidence is not a static metric. Our confidence to execute responsibilities and activities and cope with circumstances improves or decreases, and some days, we feel more confident than others.

Low confidence may be a consequence of several things, including fear of the unknown, criticism, being uncomfortable with personal appearance (self-esteem), feeling unprepared, poor time management, lack of information, and prior failures. Often, when we lack confidence in ourselves, it is because of what we feel others will think of us. Perhaps others will scoff at us or criticize or make mockery if we make a mistake. Thinking like this might hinder us from doing what we want or need to accomplish because we fear that the repercussions are too unpleasant or humiliating.

Overconfidence may be an issue if it makes you feel that you can accomplish anything - even if you don't have the requisite skills, talents, and knowledge to do it properly. In such instances, overconfidence may lead to failure. Being too confident also means you are more likely to come off to other people as arrogant or egotistical. People are considerably more likely to take delight in your failure if you are viewed as arrogant.

Confidence and self-esteem are not the same thing, but they are commonly associated. Confidence is the phrase we use to express how we feel about our abilities to fulfill responsibilities, duties, and tasks. Self-esteem is how we feel about ourselves, the way we appear, the way we think - whether or not we feel worthy or appreciated. Persons with poor self-esteem typically also suffer from generally low confidence, although persons with excellent self-esteem may also have low confidence. It is also feasible for someone with low self-esteem to be highly confident in other areas.

Performing a position or executing a task successfully is not about avoiding making errors. Mistakes are unavoidable, particularly when attempting anything new. Confidence entails understanding what to do when faults come to light, and so is also about problem-solving and decision-making.

Ways to Improve Confidence

There are two aspects to building confidence. Although the ultimate objective is to feel more confident in yourself and your talents, it is also important to think about how you might seem more confident to other people. The following list contains dozens of suggestions on how to accomplish this.

Planning & Preparation

Defining your destiny for success

People typically feel less secure about new or possibly unpleasant circumstances. The most significant component in growing confidence is planning and preparing for the unknown.

If you are seeking a new job, it is a good idea to prepare for the interview. Plan what you would like to say and think about some of the questions that you may be asked. Practice your responses with friends or coworkers and obtain their comments.

There are numerous additional instances of preparing for an interview. You should see the hairdresser before you depart. How are you planning to go to the interview, and how long will the trip take? What should you wear? Take control of uncertain conditions the best you can, break down jobs into smaller sub-tasks, and prepare as much as you can.

In certain cases, it may be vital to additionally have contingency plans - backup plans if your primary plan fails.

If you had planned to get to your interview by automobile but in the morning the car wouldn't start, how would you get there? Being able to respond calmly to the unexpected is a sign of confidence.

<u>Learning, Knowledge, and Training</u>
Learning and studying makes us feel more confident in our abilities to manage events, jobs, and duties.

Defining your destiny for success

Knowing what to anticipate and how and why things are done will add to your awareness and typically make you feel better prepared and ultimately more confident. However, studying and accumulating information may sometimes make us feel less confident about our skills to fulfill responsibilities and duties, and when this occurs, we need to combine our knowledge with experience. By performing something we have learned a lot about, we put theory into practice, which creates confidence and adds to learning and understanding.

Recently married couples may well feel frightened and less than confident about having a kid. They are likely to purchase books or visit websites that may give assistance and dispel some of the mystery. They are also likely to speak to other parents to gather information and understanding.

In the workplace, training may be offered for personnel to educate them on how to manage or operate with new systems and processes. During a moment of organizational transition, this is especially crucial since many employees would naturally reject changes.

However, if individuals impacted by the changes are provided with appropriate information and training, then such opposition may typically be lessened as the workers feel better prepared and more confident with the new system.

Positive Thinking

Defining your destiny for success

Positive thinking may be a very effective means of building confidence.
If you feel that you can do anything, then you are likely to work hard to make sure you do it; however, if you believe that you can't complete a job, then you are more likely to approach it half-heartedly and, hence, be more likely to fail. The challenge is persuading yourself that you can accomplish anything - given the correct aid, support, planning, and information.
According to Bishop David Oyedepo (the founder of Living Faith Church and Covenant University in Nigeria, which is one of the leading Private Universities in Nigeria), "Possibility mentality is the key to unlimited possibility is your imagination that sets the pace for your destination, that whatever you can imagine, you can deliver" Having a positive mindset can really go a long way in aiding you in achieving your objective.
According to Helen Keller, "Optimism is the faith that leads to achievement. Nothing can be done optimism". Helen Keller worked for the American Foundation for more than 40 years. She was born in 1880 and became deaf and blind in 19 months. She was a driving force behind many of the twentieth century's most major political, social, and cultural revolutions. Until her death in 1968, she worked endlessly to improve the lives of people with disabilities.
There is a lot of material on positive thinking, both online and in print. The essential guidelines of positive thinking

are to emphasize your strengths and triumphs and learn from your faults and failures. This is a lot simpler than it seems, and we frequently focus on things that we are not satisfied with from our past - turning them into greater concerns than they need to be. These negative ideas may be tremendously detrimental to confidence and your capacity to attain objectives.

<u>Try to change the way you view your life:</u>
• Know your strengths and shortcomings. Write a list of things that you are excellent at and those that you know need better. Discuss your list with friends and family as, surely, they will be able to contribute to the list. Celebrate and grow your strengths and discover strategies to improve or control your flaws.
• We all make errors. Don't view your errors as negatives but rather as learning opportunities.
• Accept praises and congratulate yourself. When you get praise from anyone else, thank them and ask for further specifics; what precisely did they like? Recognize your successes and celebrate them by rewarding yourself and informing friends and family about them.
• Use criticism as a learning experience. Everybody perceives the world differently from their viewpoint, and what works for one person may not work for another. Criticism is only the opinion of someone else. Be forceful while facing criticism; don't respond defensively or allow criticism to undermine your self-esteem. Listen to the

criticism and make sure that you comprehend what is being said so you can utilize criticism as a tool to learn and develop.

• Try to keep generally cheery and have a good attitude in life. Only complain or criticize when required, and when you do, do it constructively.

<u>Find yourself a confident role model.</u>
Ideally, this will be someone who you see daily, a work colleague, a family member, or a friend - someone with a lot of self-confidence who you'd want to emulate.
Observe them and see how they act when they are being confident. How do they move, how do they speak, what do they say, and when do they say it? How do they react when presented with a difficulty or mistake? How do they engage with other people, and how do others respond to them?
Chat with them to discover more about how they think and what makes them tick.
Speaking to and being around confident individuals can enable you to feel more confident. Learn from individuals who are successful in achieving the duties and objectives that you desire to attain - let their confidence rub off on you.
As you get more confidence, provide support and advice and become a role model for someone less confident.
According to Vince Lombardi, a Successful American Football coach of 1960, "Confidence is infectious. The

same applies to lack of confidence." People are often attracted to confident people - confidence is one of the major components of charisma.

Experience

When an activity is completed, the confidence that you can perform the same and comparable things again improves.

A basic illustration of this is driving a vehicle. Most individuals who have been driving for a long time do it virtually naturally - they don't have to think about which pedal to press or how to manage a junction in the road; they do it. This contrasts with a beginner who would undoubtedly feel frightened and have to focus hard. The trainee needs to gain experience and, hence, confidence in their ability to drive.

Gaining experience and taking the initial step is quite tough. Often, the prospect of beginning anything new is worse than actually doing it. This is where planning, studying, and thinking optimistically assist.

Break duties and tasks down into tiny, realistic objectives. Make each one of your objectives satisfy SMART criteria. That is to make objectives Specific, Measurable, Attainable, Realistic, and Timed.

Whatever you do, aspire to become as excellent as you can. The better you are at doing something, the more confident you get.

Defining your destiny for success

Be Assertive

Being assertive involves standing up for what you believe in and adhering to your values.

Being assertive also implies that you may alter your opinion if you feel it is the correct thing to do, not because you are under pressure from anybody else.

Assertiveness, confidence, and self-esteem are all very tightly related – normally, individuals grow naturally more assertive as they build their confidence.

Keep Calm

There is frequently a link between confidence and tranquility.

If you feel confident about a task, then you will likely feel peaceful about executing it. When you feel less confident, you are more prone to be worried or frightened.

Trying to stay cool, even while you're under stress and strain, will help you feel more confident.

To achieve this, it is necessary to understand how to relax. Learn at least one relaxation method that works for you and that you may use if you're feeling anxious. This may be as easy as taking some intentional deep breaths both in and out.

Avoid Arrogance

Arrogance is damaging to interpersonal relationships.

As your confidence rises and you become successful, avoid feeling or behaving superior to others. Remember that nobody is perfect, and there is always more that you can learn. Celebrate your skills and triumphs and acknowledge your faults and disappointments. Give people credit for their efforts – utilize comments and praise truly. Be respectful, show an interest in what others are doing, ask questions, and be engaged.

Admit to your faults, and be prepared to laugh at yourself!

Developing Your Self-Confidence Skills

Self-confidence might fade over time if you don't exercise your talents or if you meet setbacks. As you grow more self-confident, you should continue to develop your talents to preserve and enhance your confidence further. Set yourself 'confidence objectives' that challenge you to move out of your comfort zone and perform activities that make you feel a degree of fear or worry.

Potential confidence objectives may include:

• Begin a work or endeavor that you've put off for a long time. Often, we put off beginning critical chores because they feel daunting, difficult, or unpleasant to perform. Simply making a start on such a work might improve confidence and make you more eager to accomplish it.

• Make a complaint at a restaurant if there is an issue with your order. If you would not generally complain about an issue, then doing so is an excellent method to increase your confidence and assertiveness abilities.

Defining your destiny for success

• Stand up and raise a question in a public meeting or a group. By doing this, you are making yourself the focus of attention for a few minutes.
• Volunteer to deliver a presentation or make a speech. For many individuals, speaking to a gathering of people is an especially daunting thought. The only way to conquer this anxiety and acquire confidence is through experience.
• Introduce yourself to someone new. This might be someplace where individuals have something in common - like at a party or a conference, making it possibly simpler to begin a discussion. Or you might chat with a stranger in a lift/elevator.
• Wear something that will catch attention - such as a bold color. Personal appearance is a significant component in self-esteem, and persons with lower self-esteem tend to attempt not to be noticed. Make a striking statement and set yourself out from the crowd!
• Join a club or class in your town. You will possibly gain in lots of various ways by meeting new local people and learning new things while strengthening your confidence.
• Take an unknown trip on public transit. Travelling to a new destination by an unusual route and with random individuals will make most people feel at least a little uneasy.
How do you feel about each of the concepts on the list above? Perhaps some gave you little sensations of butterflies, but others filled you with dread. Although the list offers typical examples of possible confidence-

boosting actions, you may need a different solution. Think of some confidence objectives that are perfect for you - then start with simpler ones and build up.

In short, self-confidence is one of the most fundamental attributes for success. Our confidence or lack of confidence may affect the very core of our day-to-day lives. People who are self-confident often tend to have a good attitude in life, and they have a strong confidence in themselves. This conviction permits people to take chances and endure setbacks while all the while thinking that objectives will come eventually. People who lack self-confidence frequently question their talents, which might hold them back from accomplishing their objectives. It might leave them filled with self-doubt and battling with a dread of failure. Meaning their lack of confidence continuously throws barriers in their path.

Chapter 5: Turning Challenges to Opportunities.

There is an ancient Zen fable about a monarch whose people had become soft and entitled. Dissatisfied with this state of things, he planned to teach them a lesson. His plan was simple: He would throw a massive rock in the centre of the major road, totally barring access to the city. He would then hide nearby and examine their responses.

Defining your destiny for success

How would they respond? Would they join together to remove it? Or would they become disheartened, stop, and return home?

With mounting dismay, the king watched as subject after subject came to this obstruction and turned away. Or, at most, attempted half-heartedly before giving up. Many loudly protested or blamed the king or fortune or mourned the inconvenience, but none managed to do anything about it.

After many days, a lone peasant came along on his way into town. He did not turn away. Instead, he pushed and strained, attempting to force it out of the way. Then, an idea occurred to him: He raced into the adjacent woods to locate anything he might use for leverage. Finally, he returned with a big branch he had made into a lever and used it to remove the enormous boulder from the path. Beneath the rock was a bag of gold cash and a message from the monarch, which said: "The obstacle in the path becomes the path. Never forget, inside every challenge is a chance to enhance our condition."

What if you could reverse your hurdles and convert them into opportunities?

Here are 10 historical tactics for accomplishing precisely that – adopted by great men and women over the ages.

Strategy 1: Alter Your Perspective

According to Victor Frankl (Victor Frankl is the founder of logotherapy, a school of psychotherapy that describes a search for life's meaning as the central human motivational force; he was born in 1905 and died in 1996), "Man does not simply exist but always decides what his existence will be, what he will become the next moment".

We pick how we look at things. How we approach a challenge, influences how hard it will be to conquer.

By managing our illogical emotions, we may view things as they are, not as we believe them to be.

Think of it as selective editing — not to fool others, but to correctly orient ourselves.

Where the head goes, the body follows. Perception precedes action. Appropriate action follows the appropriate viewpoint.

Strategy 2: Flip The Obstacle On Its Head

According to Laura Ingalls Wilder, "There is good in everything if only we look for it". (Laura Ingalls Wilder is the author of the children's book "Little House on the Prairie") The circumstances that we first perceive as unfavorable all include a positive, exposed advantage that we may notice and act on.

A computer malfunction that damages your work is now a method to make it twice as wonderful since you're more prepared.

Having a lousy employer is now a chance to learn from his shortcomings as you fill out your CV and hunt for better positions elsewhere.

Notice this is a full mental flip: Seeing through the negative, through its backside, and through to the positive.

Strategy 3: Stay Moving, Always

According to Theodore Roosevelt Jr., "We must all either wear out or rust out, every one of us, my option is to wear out". (Theodore Roosevelt Jr. was a soldier, conservationist, naturalist, and writer who served as the 26th President of the United States from 1901 to 1909)

Those who face challenges and life with the greatest initiative and vigor typically triumph.

Courage is merely taking action. Start by saying yes to build momentum, and you'll be on your way.

Obstacles appear more scary when we pause to gaze up at them.

Strategy 4: Fail Cheaply and Quickly

Wendell Phillips was an American abolitionist, advocate for Native Americans, orator, and attorney. Phillips was seen by many Blacks as "the one white American wholly color-blind and free from race prejudice. He said, "What is defeat? Nothing but education, nothing but the initial steps to something better".

Failure is now a feature, as engineers like to say.

There's nothing wrong with being incorrect. Each time it occurs, new possibilities open up to us, and challenges may be transformed into opportunities.

When failure does arise, ask: Why did this happen? This helps spawn alternate methods of accomplishing what has to be done. Failure forces you to think your way out of difficult situations and is a source of discoveries.

Strategy 5: Follow The Process

Heraclitus, an ancient Greek Pre-Socratic Philosopher from the city of Ephesus, which was then part of the Persian Empire, said, "Under the comb, the tangle and the straight path are the same."

In the turmoil of life, the process offers us with a path.

For whatever barriers you come across, take a breath, execute the immediate composite component in front of you — and follow its thread into action.

The process is about doing the tiny things right now. Not thinking about what could happen later, or the outcomes, or the full picture.

Strategy 6: What's Right Is What Works

Deng Xiaoping (1904-1997) was a Chinese revolutionary who served as a paramount leader of the People's Republic of China from 1978-1989. Deng gradually rose to supreme power and led China through a series of far-reaching market-economy reforms, earning him the reputation as the "Architect of Modern China". Deng said, and I quote, "I don't care if the cat is black or white, so long as it catches mice".

We spend a lot of time wondering about how things are supposed to be.

As they say in Brazilian jiu-jitsu, it doesn't matter how you bring your opponent to the ground, just that you take them down.

Start thinking like a radical pragmatist: not on changing the world now at this minute, but ambitious enough to obtain what you need.

Think growth, not perfection.

Strategy 7: Use The Flank Attack

George Washington (1732-1799), an American military officer and founding father who served as the first president of the United States of America from 1789 to 1797, said, and I quote, "Where little danger is apprehended, the more the enemy will be unprepared, and consequently there is the fairest prospect of success".

Think about this: In a survey of more than 280 military operations, just two percent opted for a frontal assault on the enemy's main force.

Being overmatched doesn't have to be a negative. It drives us to discover workarounds instead of facing our attacker head-on.

Remember, sometimes the longest way around is the fastest way home.

Strategy 8: Use The Obstacle Against Itself

Plutarch was a Greek Middle Platonist Philosopher and Priest at the Temple of Apollo in Delphi. He was known primarily for his Parallel Lives, a series of biographies of illustrious Greeks and Romans, and Moralia, a collection of essays and speeches. He said, and I quote, "Wise men can make a fitting use even of their enemies". Again, he said, "Sometimes you overcome hurdles not by confronting them but by retreating and letting them attack you.

A castle may be an imposing, impenetrable stronghold, or it can be converted into a prison when surrounded. The difference is merely a change in action and attitude.

So, instead of battling difficulties, discover a technique to have them defeat themselves.

Strategy 9: Seize The Offensive

Chapin was widely known as an orator and author of works including the Crown of Thorns, Discourses on the Lord's Prayer, Characters of the Gospel, illustrating phases of the present day, Moral Aspects of City Life, and Humanity in the City, said, "The best men are not those who have waited for chances but who have taken them; besieged chance, conquered the change, and made chance the servitor." —Chapin, E.H.

Ordinary folks are open to unfavourable events and avoid problems. What exceptional individuals do is the reverse. They never squander a chance to shift a personal tragedy or crisis to their benefit.

At some periods in our limited existence, we are presented with immense challenges. We must realize that this "problem" allows a solution that we have long been waiting for.

It is in these times that we must grab the offensive since it is when people least expect it that we may pull off our greatest wins.

Strategy 10:

LeRoy Percy (1860 –1929) was an American attorney, planter, and democratic politician who served as a United States Senator to the state of Mississippi from 1910 to 1913. He focuses on "Something Bigger Than Yourself. "According to LeRoy, a man's job is to make the world a

Defining your destiny for success

better place to live in, so far as he is able — always remembering the results will be infinitesimal — and to attend to his soul." — LeRoy Percy.

Sometimes, when we are personally trapped in some intractable situation, one of the greatest ways to generate chances or new paths for progress is to think: If I can't solve this for myself, how can I at least make this better for other people?

You'll be astonished by how much of the despair lifts when we reach that decision – the power that comes from thinking about people other than oneself.

Marcus Aurelius was a Roman emperor from 161 to 180 AD and a Stoic philosopher. He was a member of the Nerva–Antonine dynasty, the last of the rulers later known as the "Five Good Emperors" and the last emperor of the Pax Romana, an age of relative peace, calm, and stability for the Roman Empire lasting from 27 BC to 180 AD. He said, "The impediment to action advances action; what stands in the way becomes the path." — Marcus Aurelius.

So, when you're upset in pursuit of your objectives, don't sit there and grumble that you don't have what you want or that this roadblock won't budge. If you have yet to attempt, then, of course, you will still be in the same spot. You haven't pursued anything.

Defining your destiny for success

All the greats we admire began by saying, Yes, let's go. And they frequently did it under less pleasant conditions than we'll ever endure.
Just because the circumstances aren't precisely to your taste, or you still need to feel ready, doesn't mean you get a pass. If you want momentum, you'll have to generate it yourself, right now, by getting up and getting started.
Challenges are an inherent aspect of life, whether it be tough times, people, or events.
Some individuals experience the most unfathomable calamities and somehow emerge out the other side stronger. Others disintegrate under the weight of the strain and anguish they experience. The same difficulty and condition one person could thrive from might become someone else's lifetime unhappiness they never recover from.
In times of adversity, having a resilient spirit becomes an advantage that turns problems into chances for progress. The issue then becomes: How can we learn and develop from our obstacles instead of getting stuck or eaten by them? How can we design that transition to assist us in going ahead instead of leaving us stuck?
While there is no clear or "one size fits all" strategy for being more resilient, here are some of the techniques that will help convert obstacles into opportunities for development and self-transformation:

Perspective

The lens through which we see our environment is as distinctive as we are. What we see and perceive to be real is not "the" truth; it is "our" truth. If the reality we live by no longer serves us or has us coming up against the same harsh lesson again and over - maybe it's time to look at adopting an alternative viewpoint that "will" bring us forward.

Changing our opinions about anything may be an immensely freeing act that extends our perspectives. Looking at the same problem from a different perspective has a way of bringing up new doors of potential. This change might help us view things from a new and positive perspective.

When we practice looking at life from diverse angles, it becomes more natural to feel compassion for other people and ourselves. With perspective, we may get closer to recognizing the lesson or opportunity for development in every event.

Honesty

To go ahead, we need to be honest with ourselves. What is it that we want? What do we need? How are we feeling?

Putting on a brave front or sugarcoating things might give the appearance to everyone around us that everything is perfect. But if we aren't being honest with ourselves, it won't be long until a major sensation of discomfort seeps into our being.

We may be able to briefly mislead ourselves into believing the pretence, but we can't hide from ourselves for very long.

The sooner we are honest with ourselves and value ourselves by living from a position of personal truth - the simpler it becomes to handle obstacles with grace and a readiness to grow.

The closer we bring the picture we project out into the world with our inner reality, the more at ease we will be. When we say and live our truth, that congruency alone will help us experience an unchanging inner power.

Having a deep connection with oneself doesn't eradicate obstacles, but it does help us navigate through each step of a struggle with greater fluidity.

Openness

When we approach life with an open mind and the readiness to go ahead - that is precisely what we will do. The same is true for when we are walled off and refuse to move on a topic that causes us anguish — we will be trapped with the same amount of enthusiasm.

When we allow ourselves to open up to the prospect of "unsticking" ourselves and going ahead - the world replies by opening up to us.

Sometimes, being open to new ideas and ways of thinking needs a tremendous leap of faith. It frequently indicates we are pushing beyond our comfort zones. This may be unpleasant.

When we take that opportunity and have more confidence in the process, we are rewarded via the change itself. Life is a great trip, and we get to choose whether we experience it completely or not.

If we can lean into the pain with more ease and openness to learning, the teachings emerge most wonderfully.

Curiosity

In childhood, we examine our environments like tiny scientists yearning to develop and learn in new ways. We are enthusiastic and ready to change.

Over time, we might grow complacent and stagnant. Our spirit might feel shattered by the hardships that appear unjust and greater than life. A method to return our soul home to a state of completeness is to be interested in the numerous ways and alternatives of moving through life. We may help change our obstacles into chances for development by allowing the struggles to surface. By going "through" the barriers instead of hiding from them. And by enjoying every tiny bit of the adventure without losing ourselves along the way.

Throughout the journey of life, we are offered the opportunity to consistently develop and extend our perspective of what's possible. We are surrounded by so many great things, people, and natural beauty. When we are open and curious, we are more inclined to discover the motivation to go ahead, live completely, develop enormously, and heal tremendous wounds.

When we are interested in how we may develop through our problems, we have more of a possibility of getting out the other end stronger. We grow more robust by being granted the chance to evolve.

At the end of the day, what most of us want is to feel good and be loved. Sometimes, the problem is to come back to the position of experiencing life in this manner.

Conclusion

The modern world has made the definition of success to be the acquisition of wealth, fame, and status whereas there hasn't been a positive influence in the world. The real meaning of success is not what you can attain but what you can give. It is dependent on the impact you make to society; and in order to do that the ego and intellect must be well-balanced as they both contribute to success. A large ego may inhibit success by alienating people and hindering personal progress, whereas a strong intellect can give the skills required to attain success via effective problem-solving and adaptability. The ideal strategy is to create a healthy ego that offers drive and confidence while utilizing one's intellect for competent and careful decision-making.

People who are self-confident often tend to have a good attitude in life, and they have a strong confidence in themselves. This conviction permits people to take chances and endure setbacks while all the while thinking that objectives will come eventually. People who lack self-confidence frequently question their talents, which might hold them back from accomplishing their objectives. It might leave them filled with self-doubt and battling with a dread of failure. Meaning their lack of confidence continuously throws barriers in their path. So, when you're upset in pursuit of your objectives, don't sit there and grumble that you don't have what you want or that this roadblock won't budge. If you have yet to attempt, then, of course, you will still be in the same spot.

If you want momentum, you'll have to generate it yourself, right now, by getting up and getting started.